FESTIVAL KHEER RECIPES

A COLLECTION OF HOW TO COOK 20 BEST DELICIOUS AND NUTRITIOUS KHEER OR PAYASAM RECIPES

By

SASIKRISH

Copyright © 2019

TABLE OF CONTENTS

PAYASAM OR KHEER – AN INTRODUCTION

Payasam or Kheer is a sweet recipe that is prepared on all important festivals and it has become one of the important cultural foods in India.

Payasams are very famous sweet recipes and there are plenty of varieties of payasams are prepared and served in all important family occasions and festivals all over India.

Paysams or Kheers have placed an important place in people life of India as they are delicious and nutritious in nature and these recipes reflect the sweet mood of an occasion or festivals, as well as they are very much liked by all sort of people of all ages.

KERALA'S SIGNIFICANCE IN PAYASAM MAKING

Though Payasam is a common sweet recipe of India, Kerala has its own significance in making Payasam recipes with a special taste and mixture of its contents.

Kerala people celebrate important festivals and special occasions with a feast called 'Sadhya'. It is a vegetarian feast with 2 or more varieties of Payasams in it with all other special South Indian recipes.

Keralites prepare 'Pradhaman' type payasams mostly with a special flavor and sweet, which will attract all sort of people participate in the festivals or occasions. Ada pradhaman, Palada pradhaman, Pazha pradhaman, and Parippu pradhaman are some of the special varieties of kheer recipes, which are having great flavor and splendid taste.

In this book, we will see all kinds of important Payasam recipes from around India with special mention to Kerala payasam recipes.

Pulses, millets, fruits, and vegetables are used in combination or separately in preparing Payasam sweet recipes.

We will see what important 20 types of Payasam or kheer recipes and how to cook them step-by-step in this book in the coming chapters one by one. Okay. Come on.

RECIPE 1: SEMIYA OR VERMICELLI PAYASAM

Vermicelli is a thin, little-worm-shaped noodle ingredient and it is named in different names based on their sizes as spaghetti, vermicellini, fidelini, capellini etc.

Vermicelli is called as Sevai in Tamil, shavige in kannadam, sevalu in Telugu, shemai in Bengali, Seviyan in Hindi.

HOW VERMICELLI IS MADE?

Vermicelli is made up of maida,water, and a little salt. It is an instant foot making product. Wheat flour or rice flour are also used to make Vermicelli.

NUTRITIONAL FACTS ABOUT VERMICELLI:

Whatever the base material used whether it is maida, rice, or wheat, vermicelli basically contains more carbohydrate in it.

Vermicelli contains about 190 calories in about 50 grams. Vermicelli contains low fiber, low sodium, but fat and cholesterol free, and it also contains some protein and some calcium.

Now, we will see how to prepare Vermicelli payasam step-by-step now.

VERMICELLI PAYASAM – INGREDIENTS:

1. Vermicelli – 300 grams (6 servings)
2. Ghee – 2 teaspoons
3. Milk – 2 liters
4. Sugar – 200 grams
5. Cashew nuts – 20
6. Dry grapes (raisins) – 75 grams
7. Cardamom - 4

The approximate time to prepare Vermicelli payasam is 25 minutes.

HOW TO MAKE VERMICELLI PAYASAM?

STEP 1: Take a pan on your stove and put the 2 teaspoons of ghee first.

STEP 2: Fry the vermicelli you have taken until it becomes golden in color.

STEP 3: Put the cashew nuts and dry grapes to the vermicelli now.

STEP 4: Add the milk to the vermicelli and wait till the milk boiled for about 5 to 6 minutes.

STEP 5: Now, add the sugar you have taken to the boiled milk and vermicelli content and mix it thoroughly with a spoon until the sugar is completely mixed with the payasam.

STEP 6: Now, add the powdered cardamom to it and mix it thoroughly.

HOW TO SERVE:

You can serve the vermicelli payasam after it is warmer.

RECIPE 2: PAAL OR MILK PAYASAM

It is one of the delicious payasams used in India. Mostly milk is used to prepare milk payasam and so it is named like this. This payasam has the finest taste and has a cream-like look and so all ages of people like to consume it.

Paal payasam is purely a South Indian recipe, especially a Kerala recipe, which is served mostly in Onam and Vishu kind of important festivals and other occasions. In Tamilnadu, people cook paal payasam on Pongal festival.

NUTRITIONAL FACTS OF PAAL PAYASAM OR MILK PAYASAM:

Each 100-gram of milk contains about 40 calories of energy and good amounts of sodium and potassium, and abundant calcium in it. Cashew nuts have good protein. Rice has carbohydrate.

Now, we will see the ingredients of Paal or Milk payasam.

INGREDIENTS OF PAAL PAYASAM:

1. One and half liter of Milk (6 servings)
2. One cup of basmati rice
3. Ghee – 3 tablespoons
4. 75 grams of cashew nuts
5. 50 grams – dry grapes (raisins)
6. Cardamom – 5 (powdered)
7. Sugar – 150 grams

HOW TO MAKE PAAL OR MILK PAYASAM?

STEP 1: First, wash the basmati rice and soak it in water for about 30 minutes.

STEP 2: Now take the milk in a container and put the soaked rice and leave it until the rice get boiled and becomes soft.

STEP 3: Now, add the sugar and powdered cardamom to the rice and milk content and mix it thoroughly until the sugar is mixed completely in the content.

STEP 4: Now, take a pan and pour the ghee and fry the cashew nuts.

STEP 5: After the cashews become golden fry add the dry grapes (raisins) and fry it for 1 minute.

STEP 6: Mix the cashews and raisins content to the milk and rice payasam content and now the payasam is ready to serve.

RECIPE 3: KERALA PARIPPU PAYASAM OR PARIPPU PRADHAMAN OR SPLIT MOONG DHAL PAYASAM

NUTRITIONAL FACTS OF CHERUPAYAR OR MOONG DHAL:

Cherupayar is a Malayalam word that equates moong dhal in English. Cherupayar is helpful in reducing body weight. This is also helpful in lowering blood pressure and also helps to control fat and so helps in maintaining healthy heart.

INGREDIENTS OF CHERUPAYAR PAYASAM:

1. Cherupayar – 100 grams (6 servings)
2. Water needed for boiling moong dhal and also for jiggery paste
3. Jaggery – 150 grams (add as per your need)
4. Ghee – 3 tablespoons
5. Cashew nuts – 15
6. Dry grapes (raisins) – 15
7. Cardamom (crushed) – 6
8. Coconut milk – 300 grams (150 grams to be poured in 2 times)
9. Milk – 150 ml

10. Salt - ½ teaspoon
11. Coconut cuttings (small) – 10 pieces

HOW TO MAKE KERALA CHERUPAYAR OR PARIPPU OR SPLIT MOONG DHAL PAYASAM?

STEP 1: First, make a paste of jaggery in water by putting it in a deep cooking pan (saucepan) until the jaggery melts well in the water. After jaggery melts well, keep it cool, and filter its impurities, and keep it aside.

STEP 2: Take a fry pan and add the cherupayar (split green gram) and fry it for approximately 2 minutes until it becomes golden fry, and cook it in a pressure cooker and boil it for 2 whistles, and keep it separately.

STEP 3: Now, take a thick bottom pan and fry the cashew nuts and dry grapes and coconut slices in the ghee you have taken already. After enough fry take them aside and keep it separately.

STEP 4: Now, take both the cooked cherupayar and jaggery paste in a pan and mix it well and fry quickly for a few minutes until the jaggery paste and cooked cherupayar mixed well.

STEP 5: Add some ghee to it and fry quickly and mix all thoroughly.

STEP 6: Now, mix the coconut milk in half that is already taken with the cherupayar and jaggery paste content and fry quickly until the coconut milk mix well with it and leave to boil for a few minutes.

STEP 7: Now, add the milk you have taken already with this and mix them all thoroughly until the milk mixes with it well.

STEP 8: Now, you should add the crushed cardamom with it and half teaspoon of salt to it.

STEP 9: Now, less the flame to half and after the content is boiled until it bubbles well you should add the remaining half coconut milk to it and stir thoroughly it mixes well and switch off the stove to stop boiling immediately.

STEP 10: Now, add the fried cashew nuts, dry grapes, and coconut slices to it.

That's all, your cherupayar payasam is ready to serve.

RECIPE 4: PAZHAM PRADHAMAN OR BANANA PAYASAM

Pazham Pradhaman or Banana payasam is one of the important delicious Sadhya (festival feast) recipe variety. Pazham Pradhaman is a very popular kheer recipe in Kerala. The main ingredient of this sweet kheer is ripe plaintains.

MAIN INGREDIENTS OF PAZHAM PRADHAMAN OR BANANA PAYASAM:

1. Ripe plaintains – 6 nos.
2. Jaggery – 200 grams
3. Water – 2 cups
4. Ghee – as needed
5. Coconut milk– 2 cups
6. Graded coconut pieces - 3
7. Chopped dry coconut pieces – 3 teaspoons
8. Cashew nuts (broken) – 10
9. Cardamom - 10

HOW TO MAKE PAZHAM PRADHAMAN OR BANANA PAYASAM?

STEP 1: First, remove the outer skin of the plantains and clean it and cut them in to small pieces and keep it separately.

STEP 2: Take a container with lid and put the plantain pieces in it and add 2 cups of water in low sim for about 10 to 12 minutes.

STEP 3: Now, take a large spoon and make the cooked plantains a pulpy mass by crushing them with the large spoon.

STEP 4: Now, make the medium flame from sim and mix it well continuously until the mixture become thick.

STEP 5: Now, add 1-1/2 tablespoon of ghee and mix it well for about 4 minutes.

STEP 6: Now, add the 2 cups of coconut milk and mix it well for about 2 minutes (half-boiled state needed, not full boiled state).

STEP 7: Add the broken cashew nuts to it and take away from the stove.

STEP 8: Now, take a fry pan and pour 1-1/2 tablespoon of ghee and fry the cashew nuts in it and add the graded coconut to it and fry until it becomes golden in colour.

STEP 9: Now, add this fried coconut and cashew nuts to the pazham pradhaman content and transfer it to the serving container, and it is ready to be served. Enjoy.

RECIPE 5: ADA PRADHAMAN PAYASAM

No Onam festival would never become complete one without Ada Pradhaman payasam. This recipe is purely originated to Kerala and the main ingredient used in Ada Pradhaman payasam is Rice Ada, which is made up of rice, jaggery, and milk of coconut.

Rice Ada can be prepared before making this recipe, but in all major stores rice ada is sold readymade, so that payasam content only can be prepared.

Ada pradhaman preparation and cooking time is just 35 to 40 minutes only.

Here we see the payasam servings of 6 members of how to prepare and cook.

MAIN INGREDIENTS OF ADA PRADHAMAN PAYASAM:

1. Rice ada – ½ cup
2. Almonds – sliced – 1-1/2 tablespoons
3. Jaggery – ¾ cup
4. Coconut milk – 1-1/4 cup
5. Milk – ¾ cup

6. Ghee 1-1/2 tablespoon
7. Cardamom powder – ½ teaspoon
8. Water as required.

HOW TO MAKE PAZHAM PRADHAMAN OR BANANA PAYASAM?

STEP 1: First, soak the rice ada we have bought in 2-1/2 cups of water for about 10 to 15 minutes, and empty the water from rice ada and keep it aside.

STEP 2: Take the jaggery we have taken already and add ¾ cup of water to it and mix it well until the jaggery to be completely mixed in the water. Filter the jaggery mixture to remove any residue from it.

STEP 3: Now, take a heavy bottom pan and pour the jaggery mixture to it and keep it in the medium-sized fire for about 5 minutes.

STEP 4: Now, take the prepared ada in a pan and add the ghee to it and mix it well with a spoon for about 5 minutes.

STEP 5: Now, add the milk to it and stir it well in low sim fire for about 5 minutes.

STEP 6: Now, add the coconut milk we have prepared to the ada content and stir it often again in low sim for about 10 minutes of time.

STEP 7: Now, add the cardamom powder to it and stir it well and switch off the stove.

STEP 8: Transfer the Ada payasam content to serving vessel before it is served. Enjoy.

RECIPE 6: BADAM KHEER

This is an Indian origin kheer recipe that is purely based on using almonds and milk. For the sweet flavor and coloring purpose saffron is also added along with alomonds.

Badam kheer can be prepared instantly and children and all age group people will like to drink it. This drink contains more protein and so it is very much suitable for growing children.

WHAT ARE THE INGREDIENTS NEEDED TO COOK BADAM KHEER?

1. Almonds – 1 cup (8 servings)
2. Sugar – 5 tablespoons
3. Ghee – 2 tablespoons
4. Milk – 3 cups (low fat milk)
5. Cardamom – 5 (powdered)
6. Saffron – 1 pinch
7. Water required

HOW TO MAKE BADAM KHEER?

STEP 1: Take 1 bowl of boiling hot water and put the almonds in it.

STEP 2: Wait for 10 minutes and then drain the water from the almonds from the bowl and take them in a different bowl and wash the almonds well in normal water.

STEP 3: Now, peel off the covers of all almonds taken and remove all the outer covers, and take all the blanched almonds.

STEP 4: Now, take the blanched almonds in a mixture and add half cup of water and grind them to make a paste.

STEP 5: Now, take a fry pan and pour 2 tablespoons of ghee to it and add almond paste to it and the flame should be low now.

STEP 6: Now, stir it for about 7 to 8 minutes until the almond paste becomes golden in color.

STEP 7: Now, add the 2-cup of milk to it and change the flam to high and boil it.

STEP 8: Once the almond paste and milk content starts to boil less the flame to medium.

STEP 9: Now, add the 5 tablespoons of sugar already taken and add the powdered cardamom and the pinch of saffron to it.

STEP 10: Now, keep it in the medium flame for about 6 minutes and mix the content well repeatedly. Now, transfer the badam kheer to a serving container and serve in the normal temperature. That's all.

RECIPE 7: CARROT PAYASAM

This is one of the easiest kheer recipes with carrot's high healthy ingredients in it. Carrot kheer can be prepared for any occasions or festivals and all age group people will enjoy it for sure.

Carrot payasam is very much helpful in giving health to our eyes.

In this recipe, we will explain how to make carrot payasam for about 8 servings.

INGREDIENTS TO MAKE CARROT PAYASAM:

1. Carrots (medium to large size) – 6 nos.
2. Milk – 2 liters
3. Sugar – 4 cups (or as needed).
4. Ghee – 5 tablespoons.
5. Cashews – ¼ cup.
6. Dry grapes – 1/4 cup.

HOW TO COOK CARROT PAYASAM STEP BY STEP?

STEP 1: First peel the skin of the carrots that are taken.

STEP 2: Cut all the carrots into pieces and boil them in steam in a pressure cooker.

STEP 3: Now, crush the boiled carrots into a fine and thick paste.

STEP 4: Now, take a thick-bottomed vessel and heat 1 tsp of ghee.

STEP 5: Now, add the pasted carrot in the vessel and stir it for about 5 minutes in a medium flame.

STEP 6: Now, add the milk and allow the carrot paste to boil in milk.

STEP 7: Now, keep mixing the carrot content until all water gets drained and the content becomes half in quantity.

STEP 8: Now, add the sugar we have taken and stir further until the sugar is completely dissolved in it.

STEP 9: Now, switch off the flame.

STEP 10: Now take one different pan and pour the remaining ghee and fry the cashew nuts and the raisins in it.

STEP 11: Decorate the carrot payasam with the fried nuts and raisins.

STEP 12: Now, it is ready to be served. Enjoy.

RECIPE 8: BEETROOT PAYASAM

Beetroot payasam is one of the delicious and nutritious payasam variety that will be loved by children to all age people.

INGREDIENTS TO MAKE BEETROOT PAYASAM:

1. Finely grated beetroot - 2 cups.
2. Ghee - 6 tablespoons
3. Milk- 3 cups
4. Sugar- half cup
5. Condensed milk (sweet) - 2 tablespoons
6. Cardamom (powdered) - 1 tablespoon
7. Almonds - 10
8. Pista – 8
9. Cashew nuts - 8
10. Vermicelli, roasted - 2 tablespoons

HOW TO COOK BEETROOT PAYASAM STEP BY STEP?

STEP 1: Take a pan and heat the ghee we have taken.

STEP 2: Now, fry the cashew nuts, pista nuts, and almonds, and then chop all the nuts and keep them aside.

STEP 3: Now, fry the vermicelli (roasted) and keep it separately.

STEP 4: Now, using the same pan add 4 tablespoons of of ghee.

STEP 5: Now, add the beetroot in the ghee and fry it for 4 minutes, and then add milk to it and permit it to boil and get thickened.

STEP 6: Now, add sugar to it and stir well.

STEP 7: Now, add ghee, roasted cashew nuts, pista nuts, and almonds.

STEP 8: At last, add cardamom powder to it and switch off the stove.

STEP 9: Transfer it to serving vessel, and now it is ready to be served. Enjoy.

RECIPE 9: GOTHAMBU OR BROKEN WHEAT PAYASAM

This is one of the simplest and healthy kheer or payasam recipe. Broken wheat is used as a the main ingredient in this payasam recipe. We will see 8-serving recipe of how to do now.

MAIN INGREDIENTS TO COOK GOTHAMBU OR BROKEN WHEAT PAYASAM:

1. Broken Wheat – 2 cups
2. Coconuts– 1
3. Jaggery– 2 cups
4. Ghee – 4 tablespoons
5. Cardamom – 6
6. Cashew nuts – 20
7. Dry grapes – 20
8. Badam nuts – 20

HOW TO COOK GOTHAMBU OR BROKEN WHEAT PAYASAM – STEP-BY-STEP?

STEP 1: Clean and wash the broken wheat and take it in a pressure cooker and add 2 cups of water to it.

STEP 2: Take the badam nuts and cut them into pieces.

STEP 3: Shred the coconut and add one cup of water to it. Now, add the 6 cardamoms to it and grind them well.

STEP 4: Squeeze and extract the coconut milk from it using a strainer.

STEP 5: Now, take the extracted coconut milk in a mixer and again grind it thoroughly well by adding 2 cups of water. Again, using a strainer and extract the milk again.

STEP 6: Now, take a thick-bottomed container and add jaggery we have taken and 2 cups of water. Permit the jaggery to be dissolved in water well, and boil it.

STEP 7: Once it is boiled, add the cooked broken wheat to it and allow it to boil for 8 to 10 minutes with low flame, and keep stirring it in between.

STEP 8: Take another pan and add the 4 tablespoons of ghee we have taken and fry the dry grapes, badam nuts, and cashew nuts.

STEP 9: Now, add the coconut extract we have prepared earlier to the pan with dry grapes, badam nuts, and cashew nuts and add this content finally to the broken wheat and stir it well.

That's all; broken wheat payasam is ready to be served. Enjoy.

RECIPE 10: JAVVARISI OR SAGO PAYASAM

Javvarisi or Sago is a spongy is a palm and this is a good source of protein, which enhances building muscles. Sago or javvarisi is also helpful in gaining weight.

Javvarisi or Sago kheer or payasam recipe is often cooked by Indians in all important festivals or any family occasions. This recipe is commonly used in Ganesh Chaturthi naivedyam also.

This is one of the simplest recipes to be prepared.

MAIN INGREDIENTS TO COOK JAVVARISI OR SAGO PAYASAM:

1. Javvarisi – 1 cup (12 servings)
2. Milk – 1 litre
3. Sugar – 1 cup
4. Cardamom – 8 (powdered)
5. Salt – 2 pinches
6. Ghee – 4 tablespoons
7. Cashew nuts – 20

8. Dry grapes – 30

HOW TO COOK JAVVARISI OR SAGO PAYASAM?

STEP 1: Clean the javvarisi (sago) and wash it with water thoroughly.

STEP 2: Soak the sago for about 1 hour in a separate container and keep is aside.

STEP 3: Now, take 1 container and boil the milk with the soaked javvarisi or sago we have taken for about 20 minutes in low sim flame and mix it well with a spoon in between to prevent burning at the bottom.

STEP 4: Now, add the sugar we have taken and again allow the content to be boiled again for about 5 minutes.

STEP 5: Now, you can switch off the flame and add the powdered cardamom to it and the 2 pinches of salt and stir well until the salt is mixed well.

STEP 6: Now, fry a pan and add the ghee and fry the cashew nuts and dry grapes one by one and add it to the boiled javvarisi and milk content and mix them all well.

Now, the payasam is ready to be served. Enjoy.

RECIPE 11: AVAL OR RICE FLAKES PAYASAM

Rice flakes is called as aval in Tamil, atukula in Telugu, and this rice pudding is manufactured with flattened rice.

Mainly, aval or atukula or rice flakes kheer or payasam is made mainly in the Krishna Jayanthi festivals all over India.

MAIN INGREDIENTS TO COOK AVAL OR RICE FLAKES PAYASAM:

1. Rice flakes – 1-1/2 cups (4 servings)
2. Milk – 4 cups
3. Sweetened condensed milk – 4 tablespoons
4. Jaggery – 200 grams
5. Raisins – 20
6. Cashew nuts – 15
7. Cardamom (crushed) – 4
8. Ghee – 4 tablespoons

HOW TO COOK AVAL OR RICE FLAKES PAYASAM?

STEP 1: Take a saucepan and keep the medium flame in the stove and add the ghee we have taken.

STEP 2: Now, add the cashew nuts and fry it until they become golden in color and keep them aside.

STEP 3: Now, take the dry grapes in the same pan and fry them and keep aside.

STEP 4: Now, fry the rice flakes with the remaining ghee in the same pan and fry it for about 3 minutes and keep it aside.

STEP 5: Now, take the milk in the same pan and add the jaggery and the condensed milk we have taken and allow them to boil for a few minutes.

STEP 6: Now, add the crushed cardamom to the milk and keep it the low flame low for a few minutes.

STEP 7: Now, add the roasted rice flakes to the milk and stir them well, and keep it until the rice flakes becomes soft and the milk gets somewhat thick (5 minutes enough). To prevent over thickness of the milk you may add some hot milk if needed.

STEP 8: Now, add the roasted cashew nuts and dry grapes to the boiled rice flakes and mix them all well using a big spoon.

STEP 9: Now, you can switch off the stove and allow the payasam to be cooled down before it is served.

RECIPE 12: RAVA OR SOOJI PAYASAM

Sooji or semolina or rava kheer or payasam is a very simple and nutritious recipe and this is healthy for children to aged people.

This recipe can be made very instantly and can be used in different festivals and occasions and also in the fasting times.

MAIN INGREDIENTS TO COOK RAVA OR SOOJI PAYASAM:

1. Sooji or semolina or rava – 1/2 cup (8 servings)
2. Sugar – 1 cup
3. Water – 4 cups
4. Milk – 3 cups
5. Ghee – 2 tablespoons
6. Cardamom (powdered) – 2
7. Salt - 2 pinches

HOW TO COOK RAVA OR SOOJI PAYASAM?

STEP 1: Take a pan and add 2 tablespoons of ghee and fry the cashew nuts we have taken until they become golden in color and keep them aside.

STEP 2: Now, fry dry grapes until they become big in size and keep them aside.

STEP 3: Now, fry the rava with the remaining ghee until it gives aroma.

STEP 4: Now, take a thick-bottomed pan and boil 4 cups of water, and add salt and roasted rava, and mix it well. Use medium flame until the rava becomes mushy.

STEP 5: Now, add sugar and mix it well until it dissolves and allow it to boil.

STEP 6: Now, add the milk to it and stir well.

STEP 7: After it boils enough, now add the roasted cashews, dry grapes, and cardamom powder, and stir them all well.

STEP 8: Now, switch off the stove and allow it to cool enough to serve. Enjoy.

RECIPE 13: JACKFRUIT OR CHAKKA PRADHAMAN PAYASAM

Jackfruit payasam or chakka pradhaman payasam is purely done with the jackfruit and it is a Kerala related recipe.

Chakka is the Malayalam name for jackfruit and it is called palaappazham in Tamil.

MAIN INGREDIENTS TO COOK JACKFRUIT OR CHAKKA PRADHAMAN PAYASAM:

1. Ripe Jack fruit pieces – 24 (4 servings)
2. Jaggery – 1 cup
3. Water – 1/2 cup
4. Coconut milk – 1-1/2 cup
5. Ghee – 6 tablespoons
6. Cashew nuts – 6 tablespoons (broken)
7. Coconut (grated) – 2 tablespoons
8. Cardamom (powdered) - 6

HOW TO COOK JACKFRUIT OR CHAKKA PRADHAMAN PAYASAM?

STEP 1: Take a pressure cooker and cook the jackfruit in water in 2 whistles, and the flame should be in medium until jackfruit becomes soft.

STEP 2: After the boiled jackfruit cools down, drain water from it, and then grind the jackfruit to a fine paste, and keep aside.

STEP 3: Take a pan and heat 1 tablespoon of ghee in the pan and add the grated coconut to it, and then add cashew nuts, and fry it until it becomes golden brown in color, and keep aside.

STEP 4: Now, mix 1 cup of jaggery we have taken with 1/2 cup of water and remove any impure residue from it.

STEP 5: Heat the jaggery with water for 5 to 6 minutes, and then add add the jackfruit paste to it and stir until it is mixed thoroughly with the jaggery.

STEP 6: Now, let the jackfruit and jaggery mixture to become little thicker, and then add the remaining ghee, and then add coconut milk and mix them all quickly, and then switch off the flame before the coconut milk starts to boil (very important to prevent separation of coconut milk if boiled).

STEP 7: Now, add the golden fried cashew nuts, grated coconut slices, powdered cardamom, and mix them all.

Now, jackfruit kheer is ready to be served. Enjoy.

RECIPE 14: FOXTAIL MILLET KHEER OR THINAI PAYASAM

Foxtail millet is one of the ancient grains and it has good health benefits as well as deliciousness in it, and so many recipes are cooked based on this millet.

Foxtail millet is called as thinai arisi in tamil and its botanical name is setaria italica. In Hindi, fox millet is known as rala or kangni, in Kannadam, navane, and in Telugu, it is known as korra.

Foxtail millet is helpful in reducing blood pressure when consuming on a daily basis and it also has low glycemic index, and so diabetic patients too can consume it on a daily basis other than rice.

Foxtail millet kheer or thinai payasam dish is mainly originated from Tamilnadu, India.

MAIN INGREDIENTS TO COOK FOXTAIL MILLET KHEER OR THINAI PAYASAM:

1. Foxtail millet-Thinai -1 cup (4 servings)
2. Jaggery - 2 cups
3. Boiled milk - 4 cups
4. Cashew nuts – 20
5. Dry grapes – 30
6. Cardamom (powdered) - 1/2 teaspoon
7. Ghee - 1 tablespoon

HOW TO COOK FOXTAIL MILLET KHEER OR THINAI PAYASAM?

STEP 1: Take a pan and heat 2 tablespoons of ghee and fry the cashew nuts and dry grapes one by one and keep aside.

STEP 2: Using the same pan, fry the foxtail millet (thinai) in 1 teaspoon of ghee until it becomes slightly golden in color.

STEP 3: Now, take a pressure cooker and put the foxtail millet in 3 cups of water and cook for 3 whistles.

STEP 4: Now, take a container and dissolve the jaggery in 1/2 cup of water and filter it for removing any impure residues in it.

STEP 5: Now, boil the filtered jaggery, and when jaggery becomes slightly thicker, add the boiled foxtail millet to it, and cook it in the medium fire, and allow the foxtail millet to mix completely with the jaggery.

STEP 6: Now, add the cashew nuts, dry grapes, and cardamom (powdered).

STEP 7: In low flame, add milk to the foxtail millet content for half a minute and allow it to heat for 1 minute, and then switch it off the flame.

Now, it is ready to be served. Enjoy.

RECIPE 15: NEI PAYASAM OR GHEE KHEER OR GHEE RICE PUDDING

Ghee kheer or nei payasam is one of the delicious rice pudding item that is mainly used in temples, and in spiritual occasions in India, mainly Lord Ayyappan devotees.

It is a traditional recipe item and so some use brass containers to prepare, but we can use whatever container we use to cook other payasam recipes.

MAIN INGREDIENTS TO COOK NEI PAYASAM OR GHEE KHEER OR GHEE RICE PUDDING:

1. Broken raw rice (pacharisi) - 1 cup (4 servings)
2. Ghee - 8 teaspoons
3. Jaggery - 2 cups
4. Water - 4 cups
5. Grated Coconut - 1/2 cup
6. Cardamom powder - 1/2 teaspoon
7. Dry Ginger Powder - 1/4 teaspoon
8. Cashews (broken) - 14

HOW TO COOK NEI PAYASAM OR GHEE KHEER OR GHEE RICE PUDDING?

STEP 1: First, soak the jaggery in warm water until it sinks well in the water and then heat it up until it is slightly thick. After the jaggery paste cools down, take it and keep aside.

STEP 2: Now, rinse well the rice in 4 cups of water and add it to a pressure cooker.

STEP 3: Now, cook the rice in a pressure cooker and wait for about 5 whistles and the flame should be in low sim.

STEP 4: After the rice cooked soft, add the jaggery syrup to it and stir well in low sim until the jaggery paste mixes well with the rice.

STEP 5: Now, add the grated coconut of ½ cup, and stir well and keep it for at least 2 mins, and then add ghee.

STEP 6: Keep stirring until the payasam gets thicker, and then add cashew nuts, cardamom (powdered), and dry ginger powder. Now switch off the stove. Now ghee kheer is ready to be served. Enjoy.

RECIPE 16: COCONUT MILK KHEER OR THENGAI PAL PAYASAM

Coconut milk recipes are always delicious and nutritious, and this one is on the line. In special occasions, Indian family prepare coconut milk payasam to celebrate along with other recipes.

MAIN INGREDIENTS TO COOK COCONUT MILK OR THENGAI PAL PAYASAM:

1. Coconuts – 2 (servings for 6)
2. Rice - 4 teaspoons
3. Jaggery – 1-1/2 cup
4. Cardamoms – 15
5. Saffron – a pinch
6. Nutmeg powder (jathikkai powder) – 3 pinches
7. Edible camphor (pachai karpooram) – 2 pinches

HOW TO COOK COCONUT MILK OR THENGAI PAL PAYASAM?

STEP 1: Rinse and clean the rice in warm water and soak for about 10 to 15 minutes.

STEP 2: Grate the coconuts.

STEP 3: Make the cardamoms into powder.

STEP 4: Now, grind both the grated coconut and the soaked rice in 3 cups of warm water, and filter it with a strainer and take the first extract of coconut and rice. Do it again and get it second extract and third extract.

STEP 5: Now, mix all the coconut and rice milk extracts into a container and heat it in low sim and stir it in between continuously.

STEP 6: When the extracted milk gets heated up, add the jaggery and allow it to boil switch off the stove (don't boil).

STEP 7: Now, add cardamom (powdered), grated
nutmeg powder, saffron, and edible camphor (pachai
karpooram). That's all.

Now, coconut milk kheer is ready to be served. Enjoy.

RECIPE 17: RICE FLOUR KHEER OR PHIRNI KHEER

Phirni or firni kheer is made using powdered rice, and it is one of the main kheer recipe prepared by North Indian people on different special occasions and festivals.

Firni is a very simple recipe to be made and liked by all age people.

MAIN INGREDIENTS TO COOK RICE FLOUR KHEER OR PHIRNI KHEER:

1. Basmati rice - 1/2 cup (servings 8)
2. Milk – 2 liters
3. Sugar – 2 cups
4. Almonds – 40 nos
5. Cardamoms – 15 (powdered)
6. Saffron strands - 30

HOW TO COOK RICE FLOUR KHEER OR PHIRNI KHEER?

STEP 1: Clean and rinse the basmati rice in water
and drain the water and let it dry normally.

STEP 2: Grind the rice to the rava level in a grinder
and keep the ground rice aside.

STEP 3: Take a thick-bottomed pan and heat the
milk we have taken until it is warm.

STEP 4: Put the saffron strands in the warm milk and
keep it aside.

STEP 5: Once the milk boils keep the flame in sim,
and add the ground rice to the boiling milk, and add
the sugar too, and cook the rice in milk, and keep
mixing continuously often.

STEP 6: Now, blanch the almonds in hot water, peel
them, and slice them into pieces (keep some almonds
for decorating in the end).

STEP 7: Now, add the almonds, cardamom powder,
and saffron strands to the cooked phirni.

STEP 8: Now, mix the phirni for another 5 to 6 minutes in the low to medium flame until it becomes thick, and now you can transfer the phirni to another serving container.

Now you can serve tasty phirni to all. Enjoy.

RECIPE 18: PUMPKIN KHEER OR PUMPKIN PAYASAM OR KADDU KI KHEER

Pumpkin kheer is one of the famous sweet kheer recipe mainly prepared during Navaratri Festivals all over India. It is one of the main recipe to be prepared to do Durga Pooja.

MAIN INGREDIENTS TO COOK PUMPKIN KHEER OR PUMPKIN PAYASAM OR KADDU KI KHEER:

1. Small cubes of pumpkin - 4 cups (8 servings)
2. Milk – 6 cups
3. Sugar – 8 tablespoons
4. Badam (sliced) – 10
5. Pista (sliced) – 10
6. Cashew nuts (chopped) – 10
7. Ghee – 2 teaspoons
8. Cadamom (powdered) – 1 teaspoon
9. Jaiphal powder (nutmeg powder) – 1 teaspoon
10. Dalchini powder (cinnamon powder) – 1 teaspoon

HOW TO COOK PUMPKIN KHEER OR PUMPKIN PAYASAM OR KADDU KI KHEER?

STEP 1: Take 4 cups of small cubes of chopped and peeled pumpkin.

STEP 2: Take a pressure cooker and cook all the pumpkin slices by adding 6 cups of water. Wait for 2 whistles and turn off the flame, and allow it to release the pressure normally.

STEP 3: Strain the cooked pumpkin and drain the water.

STEP 4: Now, using a potato masher, mash the cooked pumpkin.

STEP 5: Now, you can take a pan and add the ghee and fry the cashew nuts to golden color, and keep aside.

STEP 6: Using the same pan, take the 6 cups of milk in the low to medium fire, and allow the milk to boil in low flame for about 5 to 6 minutes.

STEP 7: Now, add the cooked mashed pumpkin to the milk and stir well until it is boiled.

STEP 8: Now, add the sugar you have taken and allow the sugar to dissolve (1 to 2 minutes).

STEP 9: Now, add the cardamom powder, nutmeg powder, and cinnamon powder one by one, and stir them well, and turn off the stove now. After garnishing with almonds pieces you can serve it. Enjoy.

RECIPE 19: PINEAPPLE KHEER OR PINEAPPLE PAYASAM

Pineapple kheer is a very refreshing recipe and absolutely delicious one. This recipe will be liked by children to all ages of people in your home.

MAIN INGREDIENTS TO COOK PINEAPPLE KHEER OR PINEAPPLE PAYASAM:

1. Chopped pinapple small pieces (ripe) – 2 fruits (12 servings).
2. Milk – 3 liters
3. Sabudhana (sago) – 2 cups
4. Ghee - 4 tablespoons
5. Sugar – 2 cups
6. Vanila essence - 10 drops

HOW TO COOK PINEAPPLE KHEER OR PINEAPPLE PAYASAM?

STEP 1: Take a thick-bottomed pan and pour a tablespoon of ghee and heat it. Then, add the chopped pineapple pieces and cook it until half of the water disappeared.

STEP 2: Now, add the remaining ghee and 1 cup of sugar. Mix them well until sugar melts. Once the sugar merges with the pineapple, switch off the fire and allow it to cool. When pineapple is cooled enough keep it in the refrigerator in deep freeze box for about 10 to 15 minutes.

STEP 3: Now, boil sabudhana (sago) with 5 cups of water, and then cool it enough and keep it in the refrigerator in deep freeze box for about 10 to 15 minutes.

STEP 4: Now, boil the milk we have taken, cool it enough and keep it in the refrigerator in deep freeze box for about 10 to 15 minutes.

STEP 5: Now, take out the 3 chilled content from refrigerator.

STEP 6: Now, take the pinapple mix to a large bowl and add mil and stirwell.

STEP 7: Now, add the sabudhana (sago) and the remaining sugar and stir well.

STEP 8: Now, add the vanilla essence to the pineapple mix.

Now, it is ready to be served at once in cool state. Enjoy.

RECIPE 20: TENDER COCONUT KHEER OR ELANEER PAYASAM

Tender coconut or elaneer payasam recipe is easy to prepare sweet kheer recipe. The main ingredient is tender coconut water.

MAIN INGREDIENTS TO COOK TENDER COCONUT KHEER OR ELANEER PAYASAM:

1. Milk – 3 cups (6 servings)
2. Thick coconut milk – 1 cup
3. Tender coconut pulp
4. Sugar – tablespoons
5. Condensed milk – 2 tablespoons
6. Cardamom powder - ¼ tablespoon
7. Tender coconut pulp – 1 cup
8. Coconut water – 1-1/2 cup

HOW TO COOK TENDER COCONUT KHEER OR ELANEER PAYASAM?

STEP 1: Take a mixer jar and add the coconut pulp and coconut water. Make a smooth cream and keep it aside.

STEP 2: Now, boil the milk in low flame for 5 minutes. .Then, add sugar and condensed milk. Stir well in low flame until it becomes thick and smooth. Now, switch off the stove and allow it to cool down fully, and then add coconut pulp puree.

STEP 3: Now, add coconut milk and cardamom powder. Stir well and it is now ready to be served. Enjoy.

ONE LAST THING...

If you enjoyed this book or found it useful I'd be very grateful if you'd post a short review on Amazon. Your support really does make a difference and I read all the reviews personally, so I can get your feedback and make this book even better.

Table of Contents

About The Author

Author is a film enthusiast cum screenwriter and an aspirant film director.

His other book is "Short Filmmaking Workbook: A Step-By-Step Workbook on How to Convert Your Vague Story to a Complete Script".

Book Link: https://goo.gl/Nwd5zJ

Author's another recipe book:

LADDU RECIPES FOR FESTIVALS: COLLECTION OF 20 BEST DELICIOUS AND NUTRITIOUS LADDUS

Book Link:

https://goo.gl/4yaaGu